100
Words About
WORKING

100
Words About
WORKING

Illustrated by Richard Brown

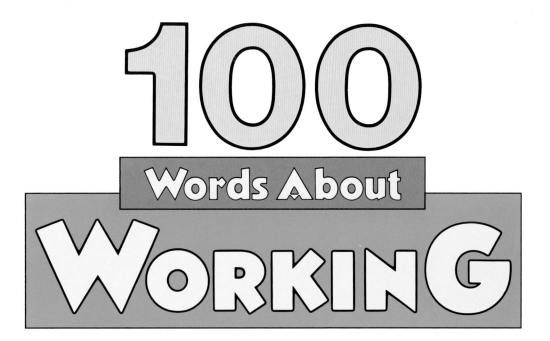

22205

A Voyager/HBJ Book

Harcourt Brace Jovanovich, Publishers

San Diego   New York   London

Requests for permission to make copies of any
part of the work should be mailed to :
Permissions, Harcourt Brace Jovanovich, Publishers,
Orlando, Florida 32887.

Library of Congress Cataloging-in-Publication Data
100 words about working.
"Gulliver books."
Summary: Labeled illustrations of different
types of work that people do.
1. Occupations—Pictorial works—Juvenile literature.
[1. Occupations—Pictorial works.   2. Vocabulary]
I. Brown, Richard Eric, 1946-   ill. II. Title.
III. Title: One hundred words about working.
HF5382.A13   1988   331.7'02   87-8363
ISBN 0-15-200553-6
ISBN 0-15-200557-9 (pbk.)
Designed by G.B.D. Smith
Printed and bound by Tien Wah (PTE.) Ltd. Lithographers, Singapore

A B C D E
A B C D E (pbk.)

HBJ

To Matt and Luke

—R.B.

paper carrier

florist

gardener

dry cleaner

barber

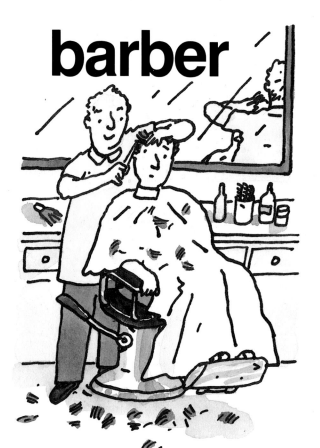

pharmacist

mail carrier

mechanic

AT SCHOOL

teacher

nurse

janitor

crossing
guard

dietician

principal

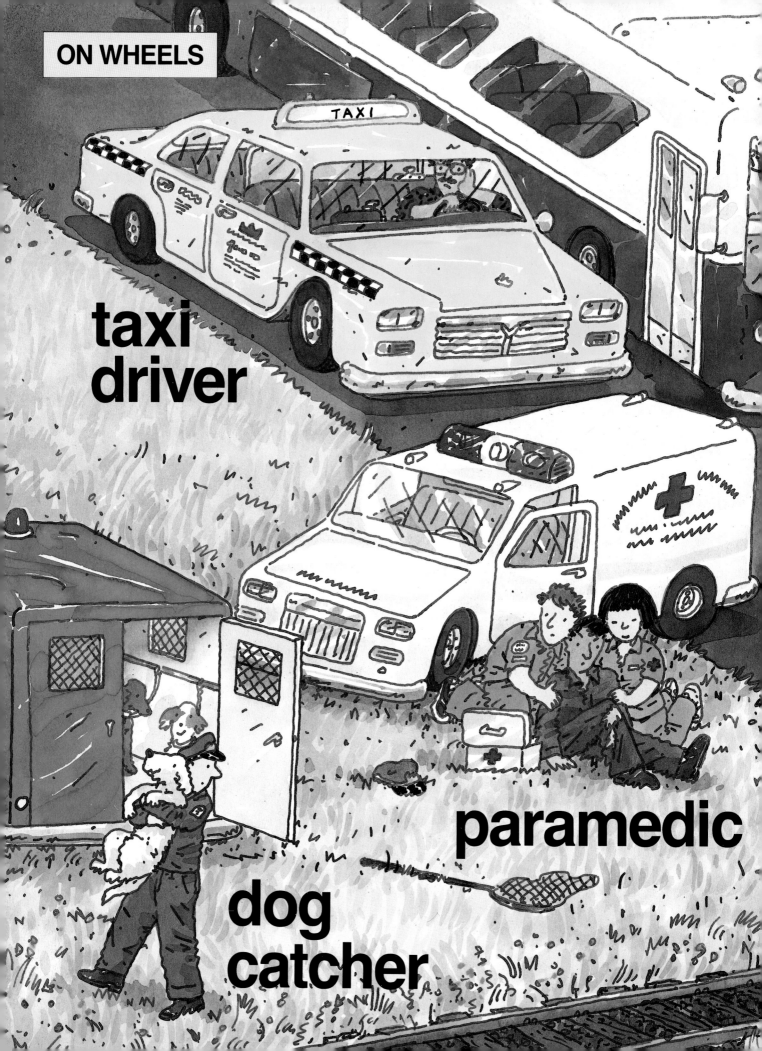

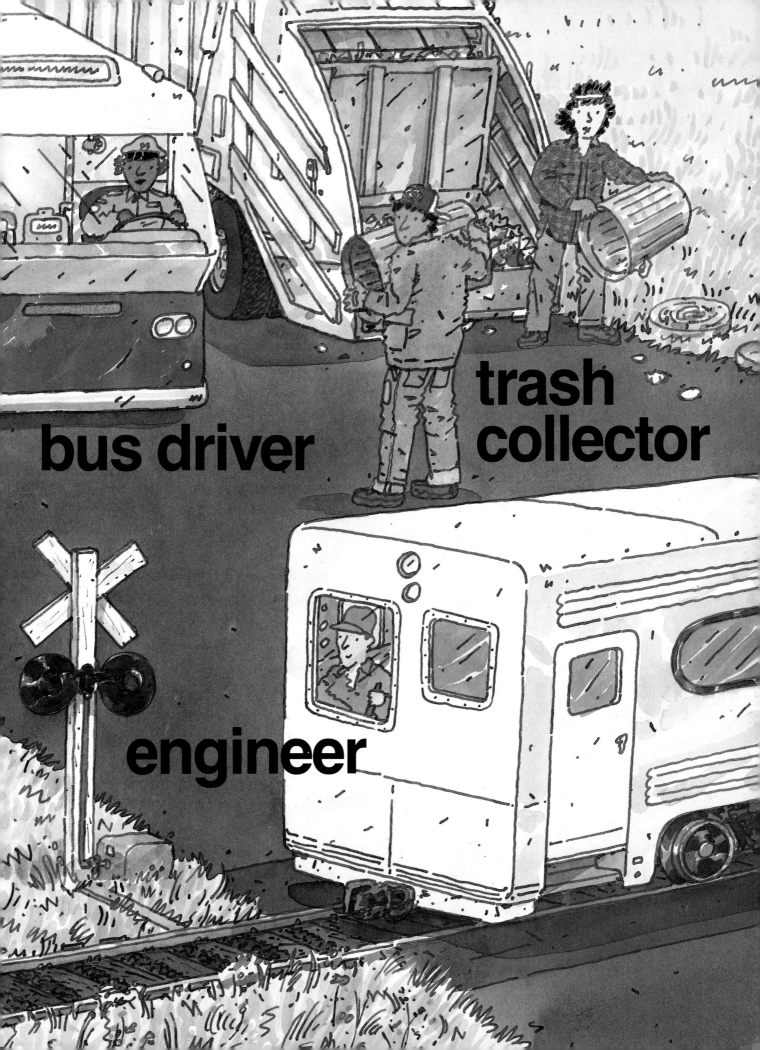

bus driver

trash collector

engineer

factory worker

WITH FOOD

caterer

butcher

checker

baker

chef

grocer

waiter

HELPING OTHERS

veterinarian

optician

dentist

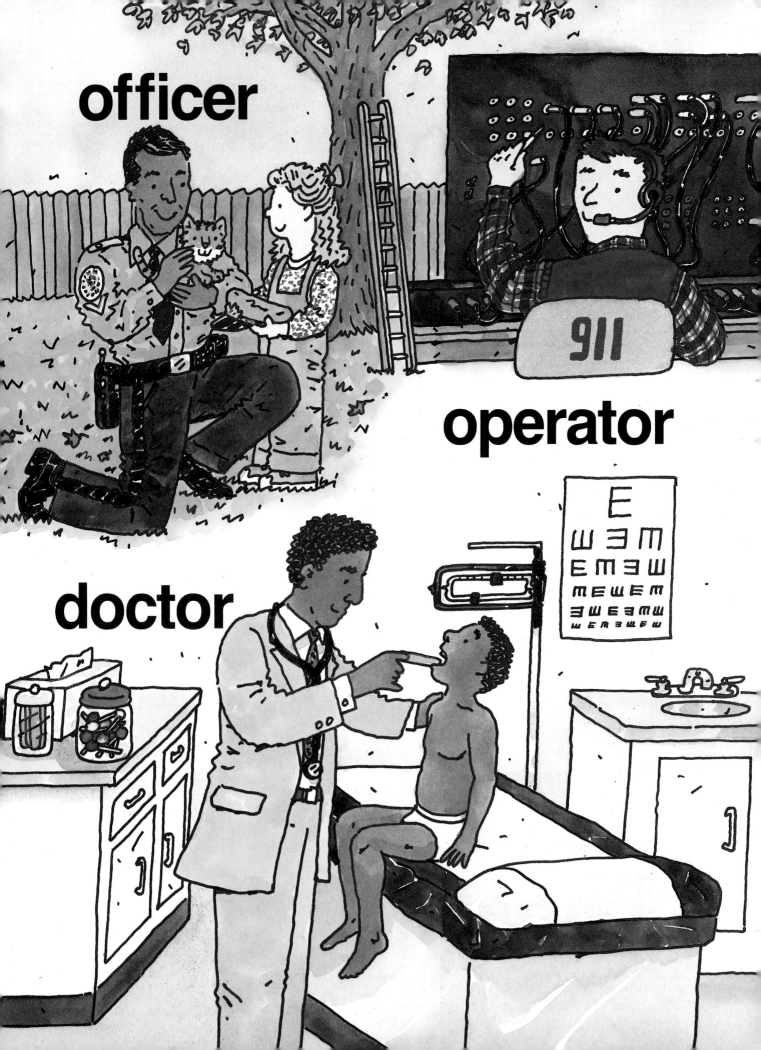

IN THE SPOTLIGHT

actor

singer

athlete

ventriloquist

musician

magician

ballet
dancer

rancher

geologist

miner

ON THE WATER

fisherman

lifeguard

astronaut

steeplejack

window washer

pilot

disc jockey

newscaster

FACING DANGER

spy

race car
driver

circus
performer

MAKING THINGS BETTER

politician

librarian

homemaker

scientist